A Gift For:

Maureen

From:

Gwene J.

It is God who has made us.

-2 Corinthians 5:5

God Made Us
Just the Way We Are...

*Isn't It Nice to Know
He Has A Sense of Humor?*

God Made Us Just the Way We Are...

My frame was not hidden from you
when I was made in the secret place.
When I was woven together in the depths of the
earth,
your eyes saw my unformed body.
All the days ordained for me
were written in your book
before one of them came to be.

PSALM 139:15-16

Isn't It Nice to Know He Has a Sense of Humor?

Y ou are God's child; you are beautiful; you are talented; you are a true
gift to life.

    —SUE BUCHANAN

G od has given to each of us an incomparable medicine bag—in it is the
divinely created ability to laugh at ourselves, at our circumstances, at
humor produced by others, and to take a less threatened view of everything
around us. To utilize the contents of that bag is to experience healing for our
minds, our souls, and our bodies.

    —MARILYN MEBERG

H ow long has it been since you skipped? Slurped Popsicles? Hop-
scotched? Played jacks? Released a balloon? Give yourself permission to
take a break and celebrate. Then press on into child-like faith and enjoy the
bounty of delights God has provided us.

    —PATSY CLAIRMONT

God Made Us Just the Way We Are...

I learned that not all people who act a little over-the-top should be labeled "off sides" just because they do things differently from the norm. You really can't judge a book by its cover. You have to look inside to see how the pages read.

If someone presents you with an unusual opportunity, check your gut feeling before you write it off. God gave us intuition that can work for us when we let it.

—THELMA WELLS

L aughter will get you through many a tough situation that otherwise would sink your ship.

—SHEILA WALSH

N ot surprisingly, one of my favorite characteristics of God is what I say in all reverence is his out-of-the-norm, off-the-beaten-path, utterly unique style of doing things. One of my delights in Scripture is finding "God in the odd." It pleases me not only because of my appreciation for the unique, but because there are wonderful lessons to be learned by studying this dimension of God.

—MARILYN MEBERG

Isn't It Nice to Know He Has a Sense of Humor?

How wonderful it would be if my Master described me as sweet, wise, and spiritual. You know, that's exactly what we become when we spend enough time with him. Those qualities, which are his, are reflected in us. The more faithful we are to him, the more attentive to his voice, the more obedient to his way, the more we become the kind of person we want to be. The kind of person he created us to be.

If I want to be sweeter, wiser, and even more spiritual, I need to spend time with the One who longs to lead me through this life. The One who wants to take me out in public and have others see the true quality of his life in me.

—LUCI SWINDOLL

God made you an original;
don't die a copy.

—THELMA WELLS

God Made Us Just the Way We Are...

S ometimes I was slow to realize that my trials didn't define me. But eventually, I learned I am free, in Jesus' name, to behave with mercy regardless of my circumstances. I learned to ask, "*What can I learn here? How can I help others?*"

And when the sun is shining on my rooftop, when things are going my way? The same rules apply—and are just about as hard to learn. Our blessings don't define us either. We can't count on blessings; we have to hold them loosely. But we are free to behave with grace because of who we are, not what we have or what happens to us.

—BARBARA JOHNSON

I wonder if either of my parents ever worried about my slightly off-kilter practices. If they did, they never let on. Actually, my father was a bit off-kilter as well; my mother seemed to find us both amusing. Since she was warmly responsive to both of us, I never felt any need to be alarmed by my appreciation of the offbeat or unusual.

—MARILYN MEBERG

G od doesn't love me any more than he loves you.

—THELMA WELLS

Isn't It Nice to Know He Has a Sense of Humor?

So God created man in his own image,
in the image of God he created him:
male and female he created them.

GENESIS 1:27

When I consider your heavens,
the work of your fingers,
the moon and the stars,
which you have set in place,
what is man that you are mindful of him,
the son of man that you care for him?
You made him a little lower than the heavenly beings
and crowned him with glory and honor.

PSALM 8:3-5

God made you alive with Christ.

COLOSSIANS 2:13

God Made Us Just the Way We Are...

O ne of the most refreshing persons I know is a woman who has spent her life in Ecuador as a missionary. Ken and I were at a social gathering one evening where this woman was present. This was my first exposure to her, and I was captivated from the first moment we were introduced.

She had none of the stereotyped mannerisms or phrases so common to our image of "missionary." In fact, some of her remarks bordered on the irreverent, but her sincere commitment to her calling and her genuine love of God was unmistakable.

After she had gargled, with a throat full of water, a hilarious rendition of "Jesus Loves Me," I asked her privately if some of her antics were criticized by her supporters or coworkers. She laughed heartily and said, yes, many people felt she should be less uninhibited, quote Scripture a little more often, and not be so prone to fun and laughter.

"But you know," she said, "for years I tried to play a role for my austere missionary father and my subservient mother. To them, serving God was heavy business—little time for fun, little reason for laughter. When I was a child, I was constantly reprimanded for my fun-loving nature; the implication was that sincere piety and lightheartedness didn't mix.

When I entered college, one of my Bible professors became my mentor. Through him I began to realize that I was stifling not only who I was but also the God-given gift of fun and spontaneity. He encouraged me to be myself and to recognize my own uniqueness; in essence, he gave me permission to be the person God created me to be."

This missionary lady with thirty years of service in Ecuador has modeled for me the joy of being released from restricting behavioral recipes. She is different in a wonderfully positive way—she's simply who she is.

—MARILYN MEBERG

God Made Us Just the Way We Are...

O ur human tendency is to keep detailed records of each other's errors and even find satisfaction in reciting the weaknesses of our sisters and brothers. We tend to hoard our niceness and dole it out in small increments to a chosen few. The grace of God, on the other hand, generously extends itself. We lean toward being selective lovers, while God is an extravagant lover, receiving us with open arms.

—PATSY CLAIRMONT

I don't know anybody who loves what she does or where she is every minute of the day. But the reality is, we are where we are, and God is doing something right there, whether we see it or not. He wastes nothing. He's growing us up in himself.

—LUCI SWINDOLL

G od's Word declares hope. God's promises proclaim hope. We must think hope, speak hope. Pray hope. Sing hope. Act out hope. Stand firm on hope. Share hope. In other words, get our hopes up. Because hope has been given to us, we can expect the best, even in the worst conditions. Praise God!

—THELMA WELLS

Isn't It Nice to Know He Has a Sense of Humor?

How great is the love the Father
has lavished on us, that we should be
called children of God! And that is what we are!

1 JOHN 3:1

But because of his great love for us, God,
who is rich in mercy, made us alive in Christ
even when we were dead in transgressions—it
is by grace you have been saved.

EPHESIANS 2:4-5

He has made everything beautiful in its time. He has
also set eternity in the hearts of men; yet they cannot
fathom what God has done from beginning to end.

ECCLESIASTES 3:11

God Made Us Just the Way We Are...

I t had just stopped raining when Christian and I walked across the mall parking lot to the car. Now the sun was shining, causing steam to rise from the sticky asphalt. A hundred yards from our car was a large puddle. We walked up to it and stopped at the edge. Christian looked at me and I looked at him and then at our white summer shoes. As one soul we both jumped into the puddle at the same time and splashed and splashed until little drops of water ran down our legs and onto our now muddy shoes.

That's how the outrageous message of the love of God affects me. You see, experiencing God's love and loving him in return is not just about living a good life. It's not just about duty or obedience. It's about loving with abandon. It's knowing he's still there when everyone else has left.

—SHEILA WALSH

O ur heavenly Father provides for the birds. What a lovely thought; he, too, is a bird-watcher. And to think his care and provision for us is even greater, for he is a people-watcher, too. How comforting.

—PATSY CLAIRMONT

Isn't It Nice to Know He Has a Sense of Humor?

What about you? What is your dream? What do you deeply desire? Could it be that those desires have been planted in your heart by the heavenly Father? Do you believe he has a purpose for your most cherished dream because it originated with him? God wants you to pursue the talents he has created within you. He means for them to blossom through your personality. Your availability makes it happen.

—BARBARA JOHNSON

I'm struck by how hard it is for so many women to embrace grace. It's just too good to be true, especially since all the love we experience on this earth is flawed. But grace says, "You're not okay, and I'm not okay, but that's okay." It's okay because of Jesus.

We need a long time to let this ridiculously good news sink in. Sit with it for a while. Look at yourself in the mirror and remind yourself you are completely loved and accepted by God as you are right now, not as you would like to be, but as you are. That's saving grace!

—SHEILA WALSH

God Made Us Just the Way We Are...

I t is a common error to assume we are worthy persons as long as we perform well. With that mind-set, we believe that what we do is more valu-
able than who we are. When we make such an assumption, we reduce
ourselves and others to objects or things. Objects are expected to perform
well; when they don't, they are replaced. If, for instance, my car repeatedly
breaks down on the freeway, I am going to become so exasperated with its
poor performance that I'll try to get rid of it and buy a new one. If my dish-
washer persists, even after repeated repairs, to spew water all over the
kitchen walls, I will either stop using it or replace it. We have a right to
expect a good performance from objects whose only purpose is to perform a
function. Unfortunately, we often use the same logic when it comes to ourselves and others.

—MARILYN MEBERG

Y ou might appear to be different—or even strange—to some people. But
remember, God made you in his image for his glory. Use your uniqueness to edify people and glorify God. Capitalize on the abilities God has
given you. Don't expect other people to be like you or to always understand
you. They're busy being uniquely themselves.

—THELMA WELLS

Isn't It Nice to Know He Has a Sense of Humor?

Know that the LORD is God.
It is he who made us, and we are his;
We are his people, the sheep of his pasture.

PSALM 100:3

This is my prayer: that your love may abound more and more in knowledge and depth of insight, so that you may be able to discern what is best and may be pure and blameless until the day of Christ, filled with the fruit of righteousness that comes through Jesus Christ—to the glory and praise of God.

PHILIPPIANS 1:9-11

You gave me life and showed me kindness, O LORD,
and in your providence watched over my spirit.

JOB 10:12

God Made Us Just the Way We Are...

My friend Sue once wanted to run away after she blundered so terribly that she expected to be banned from her son's school forever.

Sue, a devoted parent-volunteer, used the PTA's new circus-style popcorn machine to treat her son's fourth-grade class to a popcorn party when the teacher said the class had earned a reward. Unfortunately, when she set up the popper in the hallway outside the classroom, she unknowingly parked it right under a heat sensor. Fifteen minutes later, the popcorn started popping, the fire alarms went off, and the whole school—all 437 students—evacuated.

And did I mention it was November? And raining cats and dogs?

When the principal came galloping down the hallway, he pointed to the heat sensor flashing above the popcorn popper and yelled, "Do you know what you've done?" That's when Sue knew she had to run away. She was sure those students and their teachers would never forgive her for sending them out into a driving rainstorm.

She was still in hiding a few days later, vowing never to show her face at the school again, when the principal called. "Come on back," he said.

"Never," Sue replied.

Isn't It Nice to Know He Has a Sense of Humor?

"Quit focusing on this one incident and look at the big picture," he said. "I forgive you—and the kids thought it was great. They love getting out of class, even if it means standing out in the rain."

"Really?" Sue asked.

"Of course," he said. "In fact, Miss Smith's kindergartners have earned a reward. I thought you might give them a popcorn party—in the cafeteria."

The next week, Sue opened the school's storeroom where the popcorn cart was parked. It took a moment to realize why it looked different. On top, someone had added a red light, the kind that flashes on top of emergency vehicles. And hanging from one of the cart's handles was a little firefighter's helmet with her name hand-lettered on the front. She looked at the popcorn cart and did something she wouldn't have believed a few days earlier. She laughed.

Sue's story always reminds me of the role hope plays in our lives. When we have hope, we can look at the big picture—God's promise of eternal life—rather than focus on our mistakes. When seen from that perspective it's easy to see that no matter what happens to us—or what havoc we unintentionally wreak on others—we will be able to learn from our mistakes and start over.

—BARBARA JOHNSON

God Made Us Just the Way We Are...

Work gets a tough rap sometimes, but it's really God's marvelous creation to engage us in meaningful ways and to make us productive. In his economy, to work is a gift. Work enables you to have purpose in life, cancel indebtedness, and be of genuine value to somebody else. Work is meant not just to occupy our time, but to engage our hearts.

—Luci Swindoll

I think raising little ones is like looking in a mirror: We get the best results when we smile. Grin more, not less. Lighten up. Let stuff go. Don't try to be supermom. Do what you do well and leave the rest to God.

Hugs help, too. Seize the day, the hour, the moment—to tickle, cavort, and celebrate your children! After all, you have a treasure at your dining table, in front of the TV, out on the baseball field, or attached to those headphones. Always be your kids' biggest fan. Cheer your kids on. Then chill out. Remember, the best way to proceed through the parenting process is to pray, "Dear Lord, please put your arm around my shoulder and your hand over my mouth."

—Barbara Johnson

Isn't It Nice to Know He Has a Sense of Humor?

For God, who said, "Let light shine
out of darkness," made his light shine in our
hearts to give us the light of the knowledge
of the glory of God in the face of Christ.

2 CORINTHIANS 4:6

The spirit of God has made me;
The breath of the Almighty gives me life.

JOB 33:4

God Made Us Just the Way We Are...

I wonder how often we make our souls uncomfortable and unnatural as we try to fit into this world. The mold that this world would like to squeeze us into is an ill-fitting one. Instead, Christ calls us to be transformed in how we think, and to evaluate the messages that are sent to us every day through the television screen, on the billboards, and in the mall. We don't have to pull our hearts and souls in to accommodate this ill-fitting outfit that our culture would have us wear. Instead, we are free to be just us, renewed hearts and all.

—Sheila Walsh

When we are given riches all the time, that happens so we can be generous all the time. When we're generous all the time, people see it and thank God all the time. God gives to us, we give to others, others praise him and then he starts over. It's a wonderful cycle.

—Luci Swindoll

The Bible is a hope-full mirror that, yes, exposes the truth about yesterday and today, but not without improving our outlook on tomorrow. I am irregular in many ways, but the Lord is not surprised by the shape I'm in nor is he put off by my teetering style or that of my friends.

—Patsy Clairmont

Isn't It Nice to Know He Has a Sense of Humor?

Some of life's greatest pleasures come from insignificant and unexpected things. When God says he has given us all things to enjoy, I don't think he's talking just about the grandeur of mountains, sunsets, and waterfalls. It's anything that gives us pleasure and is in accordance with his will.

I don't want to allow the demands of life to blind me to the little joys that pop up every day. Appreciating those little joys frequently provides the stamina for the big demands.

—MARILYN MEBERG

Despite my math deficiency, uncertainty, and puzzlement, there's one problem I don't have. I'm not like certain pious Christians who suffer from the haunting fear that someone, somewhere, may be happy. I'm out to be a joy germ! Joy is free, but it doesn't come cheaply. It's based on who I am, not what I have, where I'm headed, or where I've been. It's a biblical choice, and it's the best option—every single second of the day!

—BARBARA JOHNSON

God Made Us Just the Way We Are...

The inevitable result of rigid conformity is a lack of personal authenticity—a phony rather than real approach to ourselves, to others, and to life's experiences. God did not create any duplicates in nature or humankind. That means I will not always be inclined to behave as everyone else because I am not like anyone else in the world.

—Marilyn Meberg

God's birth in a barn has made a statement to the world ever since: It doesn't matter where you're born or the condition of your surroundings; you can accomplish his ordained purpose for your life.

—Thelma Wells

Your mundane, everyday, tiresome life may seem like it isn't going anywhere, but believe me . . . it is. So don't run away and join the circus—as fun as it might be for a while! "Real life" eventually sets in, and then you need more than wishful thinking to see you through. Thankfully, Christ offers all of us a sustaining hope in the midst of the here and now. Joy and fulfillment are not in another town, another job, another life. They're in your very own heart. Believe it. Clasp his hand and come.

—Luci Swindoll

Isn't It Nice to Know He Has a Sense of Humor?

Create in me a pure heart, O God,
*   and renew a steadfast spirit within me.*
Do not cast me from your presence
*   or take your Holy Spirit from me.*
Restore to me the joy of your salvation
*   and grant me a willing spirit, to sustain me.*

PSALM 51:10–12

Your hand made me and formed me;
*   give me understanding to learn your commands.*

PSALM 119:73

We know that we are children of God.

1 JOHN 5:19

God Made Us Just the Way We Are...

I find it helpful to have a few things up my sleeve for those tougher-than-usual days. It's like a survival kit for my personal moments of madness. I have several funny videos that just knock me over. I've taped a few of my favorite "All in the Family" episodes. I have a copy of a letter that an Egyptian friend of my mother's wrote to her where the choice of words is all wrong and so funny. My box of special photographs of my friends and family always cheers me up. So does getting out into the fresh air and walking across the field to watch my neighbor's horses. Christian and I lie on our backs on the grass and wait for the moon to come out. Sometimes I read one of my favorite Psalms.

God is all around us, longing to talk to us, to love us, to lift us up. Make your own survival kit. Find things that you know can lift you above the hubbub in your house and in your head.

—SHEILA WALSH

Isn't It Nice to Know He Has a Sense of Humor?

While we tend to give circus clowns encores for their expressive free-dom, we generally are not as generous with each other. In fact, it's not easy to be oneself without running into opposition. Rules, expectations, belief systems, and opinions can keep us mired in legalism and criticism. The good news is that Jesus came for clowns like us, to set us free from the clowns who would cast buckets full of stones in our direction.

—PATSY CLAIRMONT

Anybody who knows me knows I love a party. The more outrageous the better. Anything funny, fresh, and free turns my crank, whether it's just for my own amusement and amazement or for a room full of people.

—LUCI SWINDOLL

You have to know that God's love for you will never leave you as you begin to walk a path you never expected to make your way down. His love guarantees you won't walk it alone.

—MARILYN MEBERG

God Made Us Just the Way We Are...

G rowing up, growing wise, and growing in the Lord, we find we're not worn by trouble and experience but renewed through it. All of us need to be touched, encouraged, challenged, or inspired. And we are meant to touch each other in some renewing way. We are all on assignment from God.

—Barbara Johnson

J oy is permanent. Once you have it, you never lose it. It may be overshadowed by human frailties, but real joy lasts for eternity.

—Thelma Wells

G od has created within all human beings a tremendous drive to survive and a capability to succeed to the level of our God-given gifts. Isn't it fantastic to realize that most of us have barely tapped into our potential? We could be creating and contributing so much more.

—Marilyn Meberg

Isn't It Nice to Know He Has a Sense of Humor?

Jesus said, "Peace I leave with you; my peace I give you. I do not give you as the world gives. Do not let your hearts be troubled and do not be afraid."

JOHN 14:27

God is for me.

PSALM 56:9

We love because God first loved us.

1 JOHN 4:19

God Made Us Just the Way We Are...

Joy is like a bouquet of balloons from Jesus meant to hearten us. Not the circus kind that float willy-nilly, but the hot air kind that have a predetermined direction. I believe we enter into our joy as we determine to tilt our hearts upward, for an upward tilt allows us to receive all he has to offer.

—PATSY CLAIRMONT

Recently someone challenged me to make a list of fifty things I want to do before I die. That wasn't hard at all. The hard part is deciding how to do them. Most of the things on my list are like flying a kite—easy to dream of but complicated to put together.

Then I thought, *Does that really matter? The important thing is to know what I want and then to try.* When you "just do it," God gets behind you and lends his grace or sometimes a miracle or two.

—BARBARA JOHNSON

Isn't It Nice to Know He Has a Sense of Humor?

> *The Lord your God is with you,*
> *he is mighty to save.*
> *He will take great delight in you,*
> *he will quiet you with his love,*
> *he will rejoice over you with singing.*

ZEPHANIAH 3:17

Our rejoicing over one another is a sweet gift. But God's rejoicing over us is even sweeter. We come into this relationship with all the flaws of a young bride but also with all the wonder, trust, and love. God, in turn, helps us to "grow up" in him. What a God!

—MARILYN MEBERG

Don't wait to start smiling if you're feeling blue. The Lord gives us a face, but it's up to us to provide the expression. And once the joy of giving gets in your system, it's bound to break out on your face.

You have a beautiful heart that is loved by the Lord Jesus. That is all you need. So don't wait until your troubles are behind you. The only person whose troubles are behind him is the schoolbus driver! Go to the phone and call a friend. Remind her that God is good. And if she doesn't agree right now, tell her that God is good anyway.

—BARBARA JOHNSON

God Made Us Just the Way We Are...

The greatest damage I've ever done to my hair happened when I was eighteen years old and just about to leave my little Scottish town for university in the big city of London. I was very excited and wanted to look hip. I had long, silky hair, which I decided was too old fashioned. I needed a new look. So I bought a *Vogue* magazine and studied all the pictures. One model had hair that was cut in layers and softly permed. She looked beautiful. I took the magazine picture to a small salon in my hometown of Ayr and asked one of the stylists if she could do it.

"Oh, sure, lassie. It'll be lovely!"

I decided not to look until she was finished. I wanted a big surprise. I got one. I can't adequately depict the fright that was me. My hair was layered different lengths on each side. It was also fried. I looked as if I'd stuck my wet finger in an electric socket.

Isn't It Nice to Know He Has a Sense of Humor?

I was eighteen then. I'm forty-two now, and thankfully I've learned how to handle my hair. One other thing I've learned is that my worth to God has nothing to do with how I look or feel. He is committed to me on my good hair days and on my bad hair days. And when I make a fright of my spiritual life—even committing errors that seem "permanent"—Jesus can wash them away. He is eager to do so and will never laugh, regardless of how ridiculous I look.

If today, as you look in the mirror, you wonder if this is a face only a mother could love, remember, it's a face a *Father* loves!

—SHEILA WALSH

God Made Us Just the Way We Are...

Search me, O God, and know my heart;
test me and know my anxious thoughts.
See if there is any offensive way in me,
and lead me in the way everlasting.

PSALM 139:23-24

Whatever is true, whatever is noble, whatever is right, whatever is pure, whatever is lovely, whatever is admirable—if anything is excellent or praiseworthy—think about such things.

PHILIPPIANS 4:8

This is what the LORD says:
"Let not the wise man boast of his wisdom
or the strong man boast of his strength
or the rich man boast of his riches,
but let him who boasts boast about this:
that he understands and knows me,
that I am the LORD, who exercises kindness,
justice and righteousness on earth,
for in these I delight."

JEREMIAH 9:23-24

Isn't It Nice to Know He Has a Sense of Humor?

Work can be fun. Don't just drag off to work every day down in the mouth, thinking things are going to be awful. That can more often than not be a self-fulfilling prophecy. Life is basically what we make it. It starts in the mind and moves through the rest of the body. I determine every day to make my work enjoyable. I've always tried to do that. In so doing, I've learned new things and had a good time.

—LUCI SWINDOLL

We need to take the time to search out each other's meanings and not treat our relationships like a game in which we rack up points. Let's not quit trying, let's not throw in the towel, and let's not walk away angry (although cool-down breaks can be helpful). Perhaps then we can hear beyond the words to the language of the heart.

—PATSY CLAIRMONT

God is personal. He knows me, loves me, and has made a huge commitment to me. It's amazing how frequently that truth eludes me.

—MARILYN MEBERG

God Made Us Just the Way We Are...

Nothing can keep you from being directly connected to God if you want to be.

When you need to make decisions and nobody on earth understands, call him up. When your problems seem unbearable, call him up. When you want to praise him and show appreciation for his wonderful work in your life, call him up. When you want to communicate with someone who wants to communicate with you and who has all the answers to your questions, call him up.

It doesn't matter if the telephone lines are down all over the world, God is always available. The only interference that can hinder our communication is our rebellion and disobedience. Even then, he is ready and willing to forgive us and to accept our call. He's always near to comfort and cheer just when we need him most.

—Thelma Wells

Isn't It Nice to Know He Has a Sense of Humor?

Too much happiness in a person is like too much cotton candy—sugary, sticky, and a little nauseating. Whereas joy is like a hot air balloon, for it lifts all who enter it, it buoys the spirit, and it offers a higher perspective.

—PATSY CLAIRMONT

Grasp the outrageous truth: God is here. God is now. And he longs to pour out all of who he is into your life every day. His life can be in you and flow through you. Outrageous!

—LUCI SWINDOLL

May the God of hope fill you with all joy and peace as you trust in him, so that you may overflow with hope by the power of the Holy Spirit.

ROMANS 15:13

God Made Us Just the Way We Are...

We are God's workmanship, created in Christ
Jesus to do good works, which God
prepared in advance for us to do.

EPHESIANS 2:10

In God I trust; I will not be afraid,
What can man do to me?

PSALM 56:11

I can do everything through Christ
who gives me strength.

PHILIPPIANS 4:13

Isn't It Nice to Know He Has a Sense of Humor?

God chooses and uses people who are willing to be used by him. Whether what we have seems great or small, God makes it much when we let him have his way in us. He took the loaves and fish from an ordinary little boy and multiplied it to feed over five thousand people. That's what he wants to do with us.

God himself set the example of how to love by living and dying in service to the unlovely. His humble birth into human form—all for the love of humankind—was outrageous! God's very ordinariness is a stunning insult to the proud, a tender delight to the grateful. Every day we are also called to live extraordinary lives in ordinary ways.

—THELMA WELLS

When I was twenty-two I knew so much. Now at forty-two I know very little. But the very little I know now is worth more to me than all the stuff I used to think was important. I know that God has not forgotten where I live. I know that not a moment of my life is wasted if I'll offer it up to him. I don't have tidy answers anymore for all the heartache that's in the world, but when I try to view life with an eternal perspective, I find hope even in the darkest corners.

—SHEILA WALSH

God Made Us Just the Way We Are...

There is something exhilarating about variety. Don't you love to see a garden of flowers aglow with myriad colors, shapes, and sizes? The garden would lose much of its appeal if it were all one species, one color, and one shape. Can you imagine a symphony performed only by tubas? We need some tubas, but we need cellos, violins, french horns, clarinets, oboes, drums, cymbals, etc., for a rich, full sound. By the same token, I think we achieve a full, rich sound in life when there is variety among us; when our uniqueness is encouraged so that we make a different sound or look from that of everyone around us.

—MARILYN MEBERG

Make your investment wisely by believing you deserve to be full of joy this very second. And you can be. Decide to be. Find out what brings you joy. Have fun in a myriad of ways. Don't put it off until you finish your chores; instead, make tedious tasks a game. Compete with yourself. Reward yourself. Make work, play. Be curious about everything and everyone. You'll get tickled in the process!

—BARBARA JOHNSON

Isn't It Nice to Know He Has a Sense of Humor?

I want to be secure in Christ, not in wearing the right outfit. Is your closet your security? Do you need a new outfit when a scary situation awaits you? What happens if you misjudge and end up overdressed or understated? A quiet beauty that you can't buy in any mall graces a godly woman. To that kind of woman this child rises up and calls her blessed.

—SHEILA WALSH

I want to be God's servant. When he asks me to do something, I want to be responsive. Instantly and always. My desire is to be as ready and convenient for his use as my stuff is for mine. He has equipped me with all the tools I need to be used for his purpose. There's nothing mechanical about it.

—LUCI SWINDOLL

Do you like to receive gifts? Maybe nobody will recognize your works on earth, but God will never forget what you've done for him. He sees your heart and knows your motives. You can look forward to your "payday" in heaven.

—THELMA WELLS

God Made Us Just the Way We Are...

I spent a lot of years thinking I had to change my whole persona in order to make God happy with me. I thought he couldn't possibly want a wacky, offbeat—even shallow—person like me representing his interests. But, surprise, surprise! He does! And surprise, surprise again! Half the people I meet are every bit as wacky and offbeat and shallow as I am. "After hearing you speak..." they say. *Eeeeeek!* I'm thinking, *Here it comes! I'm bracing myself!* "I've decided, I'm just like you. I'm crazy." *Oh, you poor soul!* But here's the clincher; here's what makes it all worthwhile: "It never dawned on me before that it's okay to be crazy—okay for me to be *me*—that I can be crazy and still be God's person." *Wow! It took me years to learn that.*

—SUE BUCHANAN

I find myself wanting to make people smile or laugh. It's a little game I play with myself when experiencing a gloomy waitress, bank teller, store clerk, or any other frozen-lipped personage. Scripture states that we are to be encouragers and to meet others' needs. What a fun way to take that verse seriously and make an effort to meet the "joy needs" of those around us.

—MARILYN MEBERG

Isn't It Nice to Know He Has a Sense of Humor?

This is how God showed his love among us:
He sent his one and only Son into the world
that we might live through him.

1 John 4:9

Let the light of your face shine upon us, O LORD.
I will lie down and sleep in peace,
for you alone, O LORD,
make me dwell in safety.

Psalm 4:6,8

Let us not become weary in
doing good, for at the proper
time we will reap a harvest if
we do not give up. Therefore, as
we have opportunity, let us do
good to all people.

Galatians 6:9-10

God Made Us Just the Way We Are...

You are a people holy to the LORD your God. Out of all the peoples on the face of the earth, the LORD has chosen you to be his treasured possession.

DEUTERONOMY 14:2

God created man—male and female—in his own image. What an awesome reality that is. There I am in the first chapter of the Bible—a woman—distinguished from animals, distinguished from my male counterpart, and literally created in the image of God. Certainly womanhood was no afterthought with God, and it was through the creation of both male and female that God has offered his fullest self-revelation.

—RUTH A. TUCKER

You have to laugh! Laughter is a gift that will get you through the worst of times. Each of us can choose to lose it when life doesn't live up to our expectations, or we can let it go and laugh at the funny side of it all. Perhaps those who watch our jovial spirits will say, "Their God must be good."

—SHEILA WALSH

Isn't It Nice to Know He Has a Sense of Humor?

God is interested in the tiniest things in the world. He cares about us and what we consider important. He gives us the desires of our hearts. He completes what he begins. He knows us by name.

—LUCI SWINDOLL

When joy is deep within us, we will walk through this life with a lifted heart, soul, and mind. Then one day, one outrageous day, we will see on the horizon the Son rise. This friends, will be more stunning, more thrilling, more exhilarating than a New Mexico sky teeming with hot air balloons. So be attentive, keep your eye on the sky, your feet on the ground, and your heart tilted heavenward. Until then, enjoy the view. It's the greatest show on earth!

—PATSY CLAIRMONT

It gives me a good feeling to create little scenarios that let me think of the people of the Bible as human and yet know they were righteous people that God used in a remarkable way. When I think of the Old Testament characters—and let's face it, many of them were characters—it makes me think that if God could use them, he could use a character like me.

—SUE BUCHANAN

God Made Us Just the Way We Are...

Each one of us has ideas spinning in her heart and head. They are there for a reason. If we allow our desires to be purified by the Holy Spirit, fueled by the light of Christ, and warmed by our passion for God's will, we will make a difference in this world.

Maybe you think because something bad has run over your precious dreams you have the right to give up on God and your hopes. "What use is it, anyway?" you ask. "How can I possibly get over disappointment and keep going?"

The process you go through to deal with a lost dream includes these steps. First you *churn*. You feel like your insides are being processed in a grinder. That's okay; you're being honest.

Second, you *burn*. You are full of anger and frustration. That's okay; God is doing his work in you.

Third, you *yearn*. You want things to be the way they were before they went wrong. You want your circumstances to change. (This stage lasts the longest.) That's okay; just hang on.

Fourth, you *learn* that desire boomerangs. You can restore your loss by giving love, hope, and a helping hand, a little money, and a lot of compassion.

Isn't It Nice to Know He Has a Sense of Humor?

Last, you *turn* the problem over to God. Say, "Whatever, Lord. You are big enough to get me through this."

How do you keep believing, keep the faith, keep the spiritual workout up? By knowing God hasn't given up on you! He has never lost faith. He sees the dream in your heart as bright as the lights on a Broadway marquee. Not one ounce of his enthusiasm for your talents has dissipated.

It also helps to know that God is big enough to handle your doubts, slumps, and temper tantrums. He is staying in your court. He isn't going to drop the ball in your game of life. And he is your biggest fan!

—Barbara Johnson

God Made Us Just the Way We Are...

Trust in the LORD with all your heart
and lean not on your own understanding;
in all your ways acknowledge him,
and he will make your paths straight.

PROVERBS 3:5-6

God did not give us a spirit of timidity, but a spirit of power, of love and of self-discipline.

2 TIMOTHY 1:7

Be strong and courageous. Do not be terrified; do not be discouraged, for the LORD your God will be with you wherever you go.

JOSHUA 1:9

Isn't It Nice to Know He Has a Sense of Humor?

The most satisfying love is to be loved in spite of being known. Don't we relax into a state of contentment when we no longer have to wear a mask, the function of which is to imply we are more "precious" than we really are sometimes? We can toss the mask and allow ourselves to be seen even when we are unlovable. When we experience being loved in spite of our unlovableness, we've discovered what love is. When we can return that accepting love, we experience a most compelling reciprocity.

And that, incidentally, is the way Jesus loves us. He knows our history, and he knows the sin in that history. Yet because of the unconditional love he feels for his children, when we confess our sin, he forgives us then receives us without condemnation. And his love is perfect.

—MARILYN MEBERG

Because we live in a fallen world, we will experience negatives in our lives. Heartache and disappointment will come our way. We experience "stuff" we don't deserve, don't want, and can't send back. It's ours. But thanks be to God, nothing happens in this world that he doesn't know about and that he can't handle.

—THELMA WELLS

God Made Us Just the Way We Are...

God speaks to us clearly. He means what he says. When he says he'll provide, we can count on that. When he promises peace, wisdom, strength, or comfort, they are ours. God imparts his word and keeps it. His words matter! I find tremendous comfort in that.

—Luci Swindoll

We're often reluctant to say, "God is good." We think our cup has to be full before we can share with somebody else. That's a big lie!

You don't have to be wealthy to start giving to the poor. You don't have to be perfectly organized to start giving of your time. You don't have to have a beautiful home to invite other people in. You don't have to be especially gifted to start making a difference in this world.

If you don't have it all together, join the club. You want to minister or start on the road to success? Use what you have. Begin with the things in your hands. As you give out of your emptiness or loneliness, the gifts flow back your way. So don't wait another minute to give from what you have; begin today. Do it anyway.

—Barbara Johnson

Isn't It Nice to Know He Has a Sense of Humor?

Do you not know?
  Have you not heard?
The LORD is the everlasting God,
  the Creator of the ends of the earth.
He will not grow tired or weary,
  and his understanding no one can fathom.
He gives strength to the weary and increases the power
  of the weak.
Even youths grow tired and weary,
  and young men stumble and fall;
but those who hope in the Lord
  will renew their strength.
They will soar on wings like eagles; they will run and
  not grow weary, they will walk and not be faint.

ISAIAH 40:28-31

If anyone acknowledges that Jesus
is the Son of God, God lives in him
and he in God. And so we know
and rely on the love God has for us.
God is love. Whoever lives in love
lives in God, and God in him.

1 JOHN 4:15-16

God Made Us Just the Way We Are...

Do you ever feel as if you are killing yourself serving your children and your husband or your church or your friends, but no one seems to notice or appreciate you? We are told in so many ways what success looks like, what the woman of the new century can do. Even in our churches we see those with high-profile ministries as the ones God is using.

I believe we need to resist that type of thinking. It's so discouraging—and it's so untrue. God sees our hearts, and that's all he cares about. He doesn't miss a single moment of a life lived out for him, whether it's in a spotlight or in a nursing home.

If everyone in your audience has dozed off or danced off to another tune, you might want to check again. There, in the corner, is God, watching and listening and appreciating you.

—Sheila Walsh

Use your hands to express humor, articulate a joke, elaborate a funny story. I used my hands for fun times when I was raising my four boys. From Jell-O fights to backyard baseball games, humor reminds children that adults can let down their guard. We don't always have to take ourselves so seriously.

—Barbara Johnson

Isn't It Nice to Know He Has a Sense of Humor?

I t's pretty funny when you look around and see some of the people God has picked to serve him. I don't want to mention names, but take a look at the speakers and musicians he's using! Some of these people are really weird. Sometimes it's the least likely person imaginable. Like me, for instance—spiritually challenged me!

Before I became a speaker, I thought that when these people weren't actually speaking or singing, they were sitting around all dressed up and in deep theological conversation eating peeled grapes.

I often talk to people who tell me they are ordinary, that they have nothing to offer and couldn't possibly be used by God. The Gaithers were school teachers in Indiana. That's pretty ordinary! No one is ordinary in God's sight! It strikes me that God can use plain ol' simple Spam and baloney eaters as his servants every bit as well as he can use big ol' brainy theologians with their discussions about Darwin and their peeled grapes.

—SUE BUCHANAN

God Made Us Just the Way We Are...

Nothing about us is incidental to God. Nothing about us diverts his attention from our well-being. And nothing stems the flow of his compassion.

—Marilyn Meberg

At times women become so engrossed in taking care of the needs of others that they don't take a moment to think about their own. Maybe you can set aside a half hour this week to write down your dreams. Go ahead and elaborate. Dream on. Then write a prayer committing them to the Lord.

—Barbara Johnson

Jesus is the only friend who understands everything that can happen to us. He knows firsthand how situations feel, taste, smell, sound, hurt, tempt, disappoint, excite, motivate, influence, stimulate . . . everything. We can feebly try to tell him about our experiences, but he already knows, sees, and understands.

—Thelma Wells

Isn't It Nice to Know He Has a Sense of Humor?

Godliness with contentment is great gain.

1 TIMOTHY 6:6

I love you, O LORD, my strength.
The LORD is my rock, my fortress and my deliverer;
*   my God is my rock, in whom I take refuge.*
*   He is my shield and the horn of my salvation, my*
*   stronghold.*
I call to the LORD, who is worthy of praise,
*   and I am saved from my enemies.*

PSALM 18:1-3

Count yourselves dead to sin but alive to God in Christ Jesus.

ROMANS 6:11

God Made Us Just the Way We Are...

As children of God, we live as though we are tuning up for the show, waiting for the curtain to rise and our real lives to begin. With this outrageous hope for tomorrow, we can live with renewed passion for today.

—SHEILA WALSH

When our lives get bumpy, we start looking around for God. It's not that we expect him to explain why things are happening the way they are (although occasionally we do whine, "why me, Lord?"). We just need to remind ourselves that he is there, still in control. And everything's going to be all right—if not in this life, then certainly in the next! As believers, when we look around for hope, we find God, constant and true.

—BARBARA JOHNSON

Remember, Jesus is watching you, guarding your mind, encouraging you to develop the habit of cheerfulness.

—MARILYN MEBERG

Isn't It Nice to Know He Has a Sense of Humor?

I've spent the better part of a lifetime playing the role of an intellectually-challenged dumb blonde, not only in everyday actions, but spiritually as well. I didn't have a clue as to what God's will was for my life. In fact, I spent years being careful not to find out what God had in mind for me. I am just coming alive—just now waking up spiritually—and what I'm finding out is not terrifying. It's so simple! So simple a shallow person can understand it. What I've found out about God is that he is totally trustworthy, and I can relax in his plans. And besides that, all he wants is—are you ready for this?—for me to be his person. Just be his person, for heaven's sake! Furthermore, I don't have to be brilliant or have a theology degree; he's given me this wonderful guidebook, his Holy Word!

—SUE BUCHANAN

I thought that what I did for God and others made me loved, but I was really fed up with it. Now I understand that I am loved by God anyway, even if I do stay under the bed for a couple of months.

—SHEILA WALSH

God Made Us Just the Way We Are...

E very day at work, home, school, and play, God presents us with opportunities to be a blessing to people who may not be as nice to us as we
deserve or desire. In the middle of these opportunities he strengthens us and
enables us to pay back good for evil. It may be as small as giving a genuinely
friendly smile to someone who's been ugly to you. It may be complimenting
someone who is obviously jealous of you. It may be graciously offering to
ease a colleague's workload even though she never offers to help you.
Instead of giving those who mistreat you a taste of their own medicine, bless
them. Pray for them. Be ready to come to their aid if they need you. Forgive
them. Show them the love of Jesus.

—THELMA WELLS

Isn't It Nice to Know He Has a Sense of Humor?

For the grace of God that brings salvation
has appeared to all men. It teaches us to say "No"
to ungodliness and worldly passions, and to live
self~controlled, upright and godly lives
in this present age.

TITUS 2:11-12

The LORD is my strength and my shield;
my heart trusts in him, and I am helped.

PSALM 28:7

The LORD does not look at
the things man looks at.
Man looks at the outward
appearance; but the LORD
looks at the heart.

1 SAMUEL 16:7

God Made Us Just the Way We Are...

Not too many of us sit around and think about the fact that we are wonderfully made. In fact, quite the opposite is true. We complain about our bodies continually—that we're too fat, or our hips are too big, or our breasts are too small or they sag.

But think about it! I'm a masterpiece! You're a masterpiece! Isn't that another reason for us to compliment each other—even be lavish with our praise? After all, we are praising God when we do that. And if others say good things about us and we twist and squirm, uneasy with being complimented, well duh! We are denying our Father his just worship.

—SUE BUCHANAN

You created my inmost being:
you knit me together in my mother's womb.
I praise you because I am fearfully and wonderfully
made;
your works are wonderful,
I know that full well.

PSALM 139:13-14

Isn't It Nice to Know He Has a Sense of Humor?

When we suffer from mental and emotional distress, God is still living within us, still connected to our spirit. Many of us have souls that are lacerated with wounds from the past and the present. We've tried to pray our way through the pain, and yet, for reasons known only to God, the anguish remains. That doesn't mean God has left; he never leaves. Remember, he is the God of our souls as well as of our spirits.

—MARILYN MEBERG

Imagine with me that a movie was made of your life. Nothing was left out. Everything you've ever said or done was right up there on the big screen for everyone to see. How would you feel? Ney Bailey, a dear friend of Women of Faith, asked us that once. And then she reminded us that the great outrageous news of the gospel is that God has seen our movie, the whole story, and he loves us.

Let me say that one more time in case you missed it: God has seen your movie—the whole story of your whole life—and he loves you. No matter what. Even if you feel that there is something in your past or present that negates the grace of God, there is no such thing. All you have to do is be willing to receive.

—SHEILA WALSH

God Made Us Just the Way We Are...

You, too, can keep on keeping on when you put your hope in God alone. You can get your hopes up and keep them up as you walk on the tightropes of life. You can swing from one trapeze bar to the next when you are confident in your hope that even if you fall, as the flying trapeze artists sometimes do, there is a net of protection under you that prevents your ultimate destruction.

This kind of sustaining hope is rooted in faith—in the steadfast assurance that what God has revealed and promised in his Word is true. We grab onto this hope when we fly out in faith, believing that God will do what he says. We find the confidence to fly by remembering how God has kept his promises to us in the past, analyzing how he is keeping them in the present, and believing that he will do no less in the future.

—THELMA WELLS

Isn't It Nice to Know He Has a Sense of Humor?

O LORD, you have searched me
and you know me.
You know when I sit and when I rise;
you perceive my thoughts from afar.
You discern my going out and my lying down;
you are familiar with all my ways.

PSALM 139:1–3

For I am convinced that neither death nor life,
neither angels nor demons, neither the present nor
the future, nor any powers, neither height nor depth,
nor anything else in all creation, will be able to
separate us from the love of God.

ROMANS 8:38–39

The LORD is my light and my salvation—
whom shall I fear?
The LORD is the stronghold of my life—
of whom shall I be afraid?

PSALM 27:1

God Made Us Just the Way We Are...

You're never too old to start living fully. Ask God for a fresh perspective on your life. Try things you've never tried before. Enlist in a joint project with friends—even with people you don't know. Neighbors. Church buddies. Ask yourself what you want most from life, and go for it.

—LUCI SWINDOLL

When I was working on my last album, "Hope," it was very important to me that every song contained this rich truth that God is weaving through the tapestry of my own life. I wanted my listeners to feel like I was sitting down with them, one at a time, hand in hand, and singing to them about the hope that does not disappoint. When you've been in a dark place and have lost hope, and into that solitary cell, the Lamb of God has come to sit and weep with you, and then carried you out, you long to share that hope with others. Hope is no longer just in my head; it's written all over my heart. It has become as deep as the marrow in my bones.

—SHEILA WALSH

Isn't It Nice to Know He Has a Sense of Humor?

Not that we are competent in ourselves to
claim anything for ourselves, but our
competence comes from God.

2 CORINTHIANS 3:5

Yet I am always with you, LORD,
you hold me by my right hand.
You guide me with your counsel,
and afterward you will take me into glory.

PSALM 73:23-24

Praise be to the God and Father of our
Lord Jesus Christ, who has blessed us in the heavenly
realms with every spiritual blessing in Christ.
For he chose us in him before the creation of the
world to be holy and blameless in his sight.

EPHESIANS 1:3-4

God Made Us Just the Way We Are...

This is love: not that we loved God, but that he loved us.

1 JOHN 4:10

Philip Yancey proclaims, "There's nothing I can do to make God love me more, and nothing I can do to make God love me less!" That means I can witness to 8,962 people before lunch tomorrow, lead them to Christ, supply them with follow-up material, and God will not be any more impressed with me or love me more than if I played golf instead, breaking my usual two or three windows along the way.

That means that even though I thought I was called to the mission field but got married instead and had four children, God still does not love me any more or any less even though I never went to Romania.

Isn't It Nice to Know He Has a Sense of Humor?

That means that even though I yell at my kids and hate myself for doing it, God still does not love me any more or any less in spite of my lack of self-control.

Can you wrap your mind around that kind of love? Do you find yourself saying a few "yeah, buts"? That kind of love is nothing short of outrageous. It defies human logic. It defies human experience.

—MARILYN MEBERG

God Made Us Just the Way We Are...

A ll my life people have reminded me that there's a time to laugh and a time to shut up. It seems I'm always laughing at the wrong time or at the wrong thing. I somehow think that when conversation gets too heavy—too serious—it's up to me to lighten things up. From the time I was a small child, my parents would look at me as though I was from Mars, shake their heads at each other, and one of them would mutter, "She's not like my side of the family!" I wasn't a bad child; I was just unpredictable, and I saw humor in everything.

There isn't enough space to tell of the times I felt out of place—like an alien on a strange planet. Then we moved to Nashville. Once here, we fell in with a group of friends who were almost as crazy as we were; and even if they weren't quite as crazy as I was, they let me be me. They "celebrated" me being me!

—SUE BUCHANAN

Isn't It Nice to Know He Has a Sense of Humor?

God has said,
"Never will I leave you;
*   Never will I forsake you."*

HEBREWS 13:5

The LORD gives strength to his people;
*   The LORD blesses his people with peace.*

PSALM 29:11

Do not fear, for I am with you;
*   do not be dismayed, for I am your God.*
I will strengthen you and help you;
*   I will uphold you with my righteous right hand.*

ISAIAH 41:10

God Made Us Just the Way We Are...

H ope is a heartfelt assurance that our heavenly Father knows what's best for us and never makes a mistake. God says, "Trust me. Remember my Word. Believe . . . and wait."

—Luci Swindoll

M y personal message for hope involves an outrageous metaphor, the bumblebee. Over twenty years ago I learned that bumblebees are outrageous because they shouldn't be able to fly, but they do anyway. Their bodies are too heavy and their wingspan is too shallow, but because God is in charge of both bumblebees and aeronautical science, he has enabled bees to defy the laws of aerodynamics. That's what hope is all about: having the confidence that despite your personal limitations and circumstances, God has filled you with his Spirit so you can defy the odds and accomplish his perfect will for your life.

—Thelma Wells

I n the midst of our stumbling, wayward humanity, God "loves us freely." Abundantly. Outrageously.

—Marilyn Meberg

Isn't It Nice to Know He Has a Sense of Humor?

M y love for my child is only a pale reflection of God's love for you and me. Perhaps you had a mother or father who made you feel every day of your life that you had to prove yourself, and so you have no human model to even begin to grasp the ridiculous love of God towards you. I wish I could sit down with you face-to-face, listen to whatever you might have to tell me about your life and assure you . . . God loves you. Not as a puppet or a scalp hunter for Jesus, but just for you. God loves you and made you for the pleasure of knowing you.

—Sheila Walsh

G od gave us hands to give and to receive his blessings. Next time you hold a person's hands in yours, take a second to give those hands an extra squeeze. At the table, bless the food and the hands that prepared it. At bedside, fold your hands to pray. Use them lifted in worship or outstretched to reach for the moon. At the end of the day, put your hands to rest for work well done.

—Barbara Johnson

God Made Us Just the Way We Are...

I love a smiling countenance; I love even more a laughing countenance. Something is so winsome in the sound and look of laughter. It makes me want to join in even if I'm not sure what the laughter is about. It just sounds fun, and sometimes that's good enough! I can't think of a more compelling witness of my faith in God than to have my joy bubble over into laughter.

—MARILYN MEBERG

Sometimes a dream is simple—maybe just laughing more. Or rising early to see the sunrise once a week. Or watching it set over the Pacific once in a lifetime. It might be telling someone special that you love him or her. You don't have to ride a camel before you die. You might not want to climb Mt. Everest or sail on the Mediterranean. You don't need to swim the deepest river or cross the widest desert.

The sweetest bliss is in taking the next step, even if it leads to your favorite coffee shop or candy store. The best thing is to be there where you are, for yourself, the people you love, and the people who love you. Think about those things that bring you joy. Go out and look for them.

—BARBARA JOHNSON

Isn't It Nice to Know He Has a Sense of Humor?

This is what the LORD says—
It is I who made the earth
        and created mankind upon it.
My own hands stretched out the heavens:
        I marshaled their starry hosts.

ISAIAH 45:11–12

The LORD is my strength and my song;
        he has become my salvation.

PSALM 118:14

Come, let us bow down in worship,
        let us kneel before the LORD our Maker,
for he is our God
        and we are the people of his pasture,
        the flock under his care.

PSALM 95:6-7

God Made Us Just the Way We Are...

I 'll never forget Joanne DeGraw. She was unique, exceptional, and charming. Our friendship was extraordinary. When she died of cancer, something in me wanted to die, too.

A year before Joanne died, I visited her for four days. During that precious time together we spent long days in front of a roaring fire, talking and laughing, reading aloud, eating, cooking, and chatting about dreams, joys, and regrets. On the third day she received the report that the tumors for which she was being treated had, in fact, grown and metastasized into the liver. She hung up the phone, cried a few minutes, told me what had happened, and asked me to pray with her. Then, out of the blue, she said, "I know a great bookstore in Grass Valley, Luci. Let's go over there and see what damage we can do, okay?" And away we went! The seriousness of her diagnosis didn't set the tone for our day; her indomitable spirit did. In spite of our sadness, the day was sweet, fun, and memorable.

Should you encounter bad news today, look within yourself. You'll find God's Spirit, which will enable you to accept graciously that which has been handed to you. Think on those parts of life that are lovely. For even in our saddest days, God is under the sorrow, holding us up.

—LUCI SWINDOLL

Isn't It Nice to Know He Has a Sense of Humor?

The LORD is faithful to all his promises
  and loving toward all he has made.
The LORD upholds all those who fall
  and lifts up all who are bowed down.

PSALM 145:13-14

Surely, O LORD, you bless the righteous;
  you surround them with your favor as a shield.

PSALM 5:12

God Made Us Just the Way We Are...

Celebrating God all day, every day is a real challenge! It's a challenge, but it's doable. Maybe not all at once, but maybe we can start small and sneak up on it! Maybe try it once a week, then twice a week, then once a day (say, all morning) and finally all day, every day. I'll try if you will!

—SUE BUCHANAN

Laugher is a universal language. We need periodic release from the obligation to be serious about life's responsibilities. If we can laugh occasionally, we can experience a respite from the burdensome cares and pressures of human existence.

—MARILYN MEBERG

The more receptive we are to the Lord, the more likely we are to have the joy, joy, joy, joy, way down in the depths of our hearts.

—PATSY CLAIRMONT

Isn't It Nice to Know He Has a Sense of Humor?

My flesh and my heart may fail,
*   but God is the strength of my heart*
*   and my portion forever.*

PSALM 73:26

Let the peace of Christ rule in your hearts, since as members of one body you were called to peace. And be thankful. Let the word of Christ dwell in you richly.

COLOSSIANS 3:15–16

Your hands shaped me and made me, O LORD.

JOB 10:8

God Made Us Just the Way We Are...

I have no trouble at all being sure about God; it's me I can't be sure of. Some days I can't be sure of anything. Some days, even though I feel very sure and self-confident, I end up falling on my face. Then there are the times I think I'm a "perfect-me" Christian and I fail. Oh, how I fail! My imperfections (and you have no idea how many there are) remind me that he is perfect, he is righteous, and that even though I don't deserve it, I am made righteous in him!

—SUE BUCHANAN

There is nothing average about the God we know, the Father we long to serve. He's unconventional and exorbitant. He's extravagant in his giving. He's unrestrained in his love for us. In fact, God is extraordinary in every way. He's outrageous! Let's let our everyday lives be invaded and transformed by this loving, gracious, wonderful, perfectly outrageous God.

—LUCI SWINDOLL

For me, relaxing in God's peace means letting go of the "c" word: CONTROL. Scripture tells us to be anxious about nothing, to leave our lives in his hands.

—SHEILA WALSH

Isn't It Nice to Know He Has a Sense of Humor?

E verybody who is a child of God has a heavenly Father who exceeds all expectations and imagination.

—Luci Swindoll

I 'm free from trying to be good enough to win God's favor, free from following rigid rules designed to produce good behavior, free from the guilt and shame stemming from impulses that keep reminding me I'm a mess, free from the pressure to perform perfectly, free to love myself in spite of myself, free to relax in his presence and even marvel that he actually enjoys me.

—Marilyn Meberg

W hen in doubt about your need to be saved, just check what's out of place in your life. It could be decorations that won't stay put, interests that become fetishes, or some less-than-bright action you've taken. Fortunately, even if something falls on our noodle or if we fall on our behind God's everlasting arms pick us up, and he embraces us with his loving-kindness.

—Patsy Clairmont

God Made Us Just the Way We Are...

L adies come to the Women of Faith conferences with all kinds of issues and situations. Some come with their own agendas. And a few of them seem to be a little over-the-top. You know, their compass seems to be headed in the opposite direction from the rest of the world.

That's the impression T.J. gave at a conference earlier this year. While other women were applauding, T.J. waved a white, size 44D, lace brassiere in the air, as high as she could.

She had come with a busload of ladies from her church, but some of these fellow travelers were embarrassed by her. Her pastor's wife vowed to take that thing away from T.J. But she wasn't giving it up easily. Instead of handing over the bra, she swirled it in the air and yelled "Hallelujah" at the top of her voice. All her parish pals could do was act as if they didn't know her.

I met T.J. when she ran up to my book table during a break with the big bra in hand and enthusiastically insisted, "Sign my bra! Please sign my bra! I want you to sign it right here!"

I looked at her in shock. I have signed T-shirts, books, audio-cassette and CD covers, brochures, programs, bumblebee pin cards, etc. But bras, never. I thought, *If T.J. has the nerve to sling a bra around in front of*

Isn't It Nice to Know He Has a Sense of Humor?

thousands of women and then ask me to autograph it, that's the least I can do. I signed it, "My cup runneth over!" Okay, so you think my compass is as misdirected as T.J.'s. I saw it all as great fun. T.J. certainly seemed to be having a good time. That autographing moment was the beginning of a wonderful relationship that has included spiritual growth and renewal for me.

—THELMA WELLS

> *You prepare a table before me*
> *   in the presence of my enemies.*
> *You anoint my head with oil;*
> *   my cup overflows.*
> *Surely goodness and love will follow me*
> *   all the days of my life,*
> *and I will dwell in the house of the LORD*
> *   forever.*

PSALM 23:5–6

God Made Us Just the Way We Are...

I t makes me sad to think there are women in their seventies who have spent a lifetime of energy holding back instead of letting go. And it's probably because years ago someone pronounced a disapproving "Tsk, Tsk," and it became a curse on their lives. I was a victim of the tsk-tsk-ers! Let's put up signs in our churches that say, "No tsk-tsk-ing!" "No finger wagging!" "No disparaging words!" No 'looks' (you know the kind) allowed here!" "No squelching of personalities and/or ideas!" "No put-downs permitted on the premises!" and "Only encouraging words spoken here." For me, maybe a sign that says "Stick a sock in it!" would be good.

—SUE BUCHANAN

A s Christ's followers, we shouldn't be surprised that our lives will take some outrageous twists and turns, or that we will sometimes stand out as "circus freaks" in a world that doesn't recognize our glorious nature in Christ.

—LUCI SWINDOLL

Isn't It Nice to Know He Has a Sense of Humor?

In your hearts set apart Christ as Lord.

1 PETER 3:15

LORD, you have been our dwelling place
throughout all generations.
Before the mountains were born
or you brought forth the earth and the world,
from everlasting to everlasting you are God.

PSALM 90:1-2

One thing God has spoken,
two things have I heard:
that you, O God, are strong,
and that you, O LORD, are loving.
Surely you will reward each person
according to what he has done.

PSALM 62:11-12

God Made Us Just the Way We Are...

Lord, how can you love me,
Odd as I am?
Rattled and railing and flailing my hands?
How can you claim me, Lord,
Weary and worn,
Beaten, defeated, belittled, and scorned?
How can you need me, Lord,
Helpless and frail,
Senile, demented, frightened, and pale?
How could you die for me,
Worthless and stained,
Arrogant, sinful, thoughtless, and vain?
How, Lord—
How could you? . . .
What?
What's that you say?
Not because, child—in spite of.
I love you anyway.

—ANN LUNA

Isn't It Nice to Know He Has a Sense of Humor?

I don't know about you, but I'm susceptible to viewing the lives of others from afar and believing their existence is easier, calmer, and more meaningful than mine—rather paradisiacal. Not all the time, mind you, but I do have those moments when I give way to envy because I'm trudging through a dreary season while someone else seems to be skipping down a well-lit path. But I guess peeking over the fence at the greener grass is part of our human tendency.

—PATSY CLAIRMONT

Girlfriendship can enhance all other relationships. The "getting away" for most women is rarely to an exotic island; it's more likely to be to a church retreat or maybe to the park for a picnic; but this experience—time to compare notes, learn from each other, redefine priorities, and yes, cry on each other's shoulders—invigorates and energizes us to be better wives and mothers.

—SUE BUCHANAN

Life is full of choices every minute of the day. I choose to never have a bad day. I cannot prevent the perplexities of life, but I can choose how I respond to them.

—THELMA WELLS

God Made Us Just the Way We Are...

We all have the capacity for fun and laughter. We do not all have the same abilities in creating humor—we are not all stand-up comics, but we can all laugh. Many of us, however, need to be released from the bondage of our circumstances and ourselves so that the inherent capacity to laugh, which lives in us all, can bubble to the surface and carry us through those times that are tension-producing and spirit-breaking.

—MARILYN MEBERG

I try not to compare myself to others anymore. How different I am from most of my friends. The way I dress, how I do my hair, the way I decorate our house—my mother called it Gypsy—so many things! It took me a long time to understand that God didn't make a mistake when he made me; he did it on purpose!

—SUE BUCHANAN

Isn't It Nice to Know He Has a Sense of Humor?

Think of what you were when you were called. Not many of you were wise by human standards; not many were influential; not many were of noble birth. But God chose the foolish things of the world to shame the wise; God chose the weak things of the world to shame the strong. He chose the lowly things of this world and the despised things—and the things that are not—to nullify the things that are, so that no one may boast before him. It is because of him that you are in Christ Jesus, who has become for us wisdom from God.

1 Corinthians 1:26-30

God Made Us Just the Way We Are...

A few days before Christmas last year I went to my regular nail girl for a fill-in and polish. She's a darling Vietnamese woman who knows only a few words of English, every one of which she used that day to try to convince me to let her paint Christmas decorations on my nails.

"No! No fhan-cy nail! No want fhan-cy nail." (When did I live in Vietnam?) I tried my best to retrieve my hand. Too late! She was already at work. Her stunning black eyes danced as she airbrushed a Christmas tree, truly a work of art, while I tried (in two languages and three religions, for heaven's sake!) to convince her this wasn't my thing.

The Christmas tree on my pointer finger turned out to be quite a conversation piece—as if my friends need a conversation piece! I like that about my friends, and I like the fact that you don't have to apologize for who you are or what you think. You can discuss anything and everything and know you won't be judged. You can have a Christmas tree painted on your fingernail and your friends will say, "How like our Sue. She's nuts, but we love her!"

—SUE BUCHANAN

Isn't It Nice to Know He Has a Sense of Humor?

God never views us as objects. He views us as valued, honored, deeply loved members of his creation. We don't have to perform for him—we serve him, and when we serve him out of love and gratitude, there is no sense of duty, obligation, or performance. Being the recipients of such unconditional love and regard can release us to experience the joy of loving God in return. That joyful loving produces healing for our soul. That healing gives birth to the laugh impulse.

—MARILYN MEBERG

I'm not politically correct; I don't mind being teased about being a dumb blonde. It's being treated like a dumb blonde I don't like! I can play the dumb blonde to the hilt when I'm in the mood, but I don't much like it pushed down my throat.

When God implies that we need to have our heads examined, he isn't talking about checking for blonde hair or brilliance (thank heavens); he's looking for a person whose commitment is to "walk continually in God's truth."

—SUE BUCHANAN

God Made Us Just the Way We Are...

Let love and faithfulness never leave you;
bind them around your neck,
write them on the tablet of your heart.
Then you will win favor and a good name
in the sight of God and man.

PROVERBS 3:3-4

Acknowledge the God of your father, and
serve him with wholehearted devotion and with a
willing mind, for the LORD searches every heart and
understands every motive behind the thoughts.
If you seek him, he will be found by you.

1 CHRONICLES 28:9

Isn't It Nice to Know He Has a Sense of Humor?

My hair isn't gray, but my belt has had to cut me a little slack the last few years. As each birthday party comes, I try to be cool. But when my husband, Bill, lit the candles on my last Big-0 celebration, the young people started to sing "Kumbaya." (They thought it was a bonfire!). Then, when I noticed recently that one of the throw pillows on my bed was a hot water bottle, I had to admit maybe I am . . . well, maturing.

God's Word says being tired, regardless of our age, isn't an issue if we wait on him. I've been waiting on the Lord a good many years and have discovered that wherever he is, joy is happening. I'll never be too old for that.

—Barbara Johnson

Do your work as unto the Lord. And do it with gusto! What are you going to be when you grow up? Whatever it is, people like me will be deeply indebted to you for your service. When you go to work today, thank the Lord for the meaningful work you have and for your opportunity to help others. Give 'em a smile.

—Luci Swindoll

God Made Us Just the Way We Are...

When you find yourself looking at a bank balance that couldn't keep a goldfish afloat, remember who you are. Your Father knows every need before you even voice it. He knows every unexpected turn of events. We are told by Paul to be anxious about nothing. "Nothing" is a pretty conclusive word. No thing, no part, no portion.

Whatever is weighing you down, stop what you're doing (which I guess at the moment is reading!) and with thanksgiving on your lips, bring your requests to God.

—SHEILA WALSH

Glimpsing God's heart makes me want to do back flips while swinging from a trapeze. Trust me, these are not natural feelings for this clown! But then, his is not a natural love. Instead, the Lord's supernatural nature allows us to do things way outside our comfort zone—like love the unlovely, which was what Christ did when he died for us. Now we are called to live lovingly for him.

—PATSY CLAIRMONT

Bringing God into your reality means being fully present in the moment—not wishing you were somewhere you used to be or somewhere you hope to be.

—LUCI SWINDOLL

Isn't It Nice to Know He Has a Sense of Humor?

More often than not we maintain a veneer of acceptability in our daily lives that belies how we really are. We figure out where we are going to be and what is expected of us, and then we follow the approved behavior for that situation. However, if we all follow the various recipes too closely, we become like little cutout figures, looking alike and behaving alike. That kind of conformity is stifling to our spirits; it produces dry bones by robbing us of our uniqueness and individuality. Making sure we are conforming to all the behavioral recipes, looking at and behaving like everyone, fearing we may "stick out in a crowd," produces tension. That tension reduces our inclination to relax and have fun.

—MARILYN MEBERG

Have you noticed how much easier it is to carry someone else's burden rather than your own? When we take our eyes off our own needs and reach out to someone else, we often find our prayers were answered when we weren't looking.

—SHEILA WALSH

God Made Us Just the Way We Are...

The eyes of the LORD range throughout
the earth to strengthen those whose hearts
are fully committed to him.

2 CHRONICLES 16:9

The LORD has done great things for us,
and we are filled with joy.

PSALM 126:3

There are different kinds of gifts, but the same Spirit.
There are different kinds of service, but the same Lord.
There are different kinds of working, but the same
God works all of them in all men.

1 CORINTHIANS 12:4-6

Isn't It Nice to Know He Has a Sense of Humor?

While I admire the outward beauty of my close friends, the thing that draws me to them and keeps me holding on for dear life is that each of them possesses an inner beauty that comes from knowing God intimately. Their true beauty comes from being deeply rooted in him, and their quest for a deeper knowledge of his precepts compels me to dwell more on my inner self rather than on the outward appearance.

—SUE BUCHANAN

The ability to laugh over unexpected and unwanted experiences that threaten to get the best of us enables us to change our perspective. Putting this philosophy into practice means that when something goes wrong, instead of being victimized by it, we lighten up, take the situation less seriously, and see if there isn't a laugh to be found somewhere. When we are able to do this, we are in control of our situation instead of our situation being in control of us.

—MARILYN MEBERG

God Made Us Just the Way We Are...

When we trust in God alone, life may still shake us up, but our spirit will be safe in the net of his love.

—THELMA WELLS

There's no question about God giving us outrageous hope. Hope enables us to feel the intangible, imagine the invisible, and achieve the impossible. We believe God keeps his promises, and with confidence we wait for them to be fulfilled.

—LUCI SWINDOLL

Can anything good come out of illegitimacy and poverty? You'd better believe it, baby! God knew that one day I would be talking to you, sharing his extraordinary plan to redeem and use each and every one of us. In spite of the circumstances of my birth, I was not a mistake. My sainted great-grandmother, who raised me from the time I was two years old, made sure I knew this crucial truth. "Baby," she said, "there was never a seed planted in a mother's womb that God didn't know about and have special plans for. You just remember that. You are somebody!"

—THELMA WELLS

Isn't It Nice to Know He Has a Sense of Humor?

Praise the LORD, O my soul,
*   and forget not all his benefits—*
who forgives all your sins
*   and heals all your diseases,*
who redeems your life from the pit
*   and crowns you with love and compassion,*
who satisfies your desires with good things so that
*   your youth is renewed like the eagle's.*

PSALM 103:2–5

God has combined the members of the body and has given greater honor to the parts that lacked it, so that there should be no division in the body, but that its parts should have equal concern for each other. If one part suffers, every part suffers with it; if one part is honored, every part rejoices with it.

1 CORINTHIANS 12:24–26

God Made Us Just the Way We Are...

I need continuing grace in my life today. In fact, I long for it. For in grace's company, I feel humbly clean, fully accepted, and totally safe. But I must confess I'm a novice grace-giver, which is why I can't wait to hear my friends insights on this mysterious, holy quality of Christ's. Grace. What an outrageous concept! Hooray, even clowns are invited! Come, skip along with me, and grasp grace for yourself.

—Patsy Clairmont

Decide which cares you can live without. Then toss them, one at a time, into a river, over the side of cliff, or into a trash can. Watch them float or fall away. Think about how God formed us, sin deformed us, and Jesus transforms us. Your heart will be lighter on the way home.

Don't be upset if later those same worries settle back on your front porch. Let them bring you to your knees again. Instead of shouting, "Panic! Stress! Chaos!" think, *Just another routine day full of opportunities to get close to God.* Smile. If, even in worries, you stay next to God and his grace, you won't have to say much—it'll show on your face. Don't get stressed out, get blessed out!

—Barbara Johnson

Isn't It Nice to Know He Has a Sense of Humor?

You have made known to me the path of life;
you will fill me with joy in your presence,
with eternal pleasures at your right hand.

PSALM 16:11

I will put my Spirit in you and you will live.
Then you will know that I the LORD
have spoken and I have done it.

EZEKIEL 37:14

When times are good, be happy;
but when times are bad, consider:
God has made the one
as well as the other.

ECCLESIASTES 7:14

God Made Us Just the Way We Are...

S ometimes when we forget ourselves and focus on the needs of another, God answers our deepest prayers.

—SHEILA WALSH

G od's family is made up of all sorts of "worker bees." Some make work look like play—the ones who are always front and center. They sing, play instruments, perform drama, preach, and teach. Then there are those whose work really looks like work! They dish soup to the poor, tutor kids in the inner city, build homes for the less fortunate, work in church kitchens, or do the janitor work at church.

Whatever the job is that God has called you and me to do, he wants us to go at it like there's no tomorrow—with all our hearts!

—SUE BUCHANAN

G od loves us too much to leave us muddling about in our sin. No matter what our problem—lying, cheating, marital unfaithfulness, yelling at the kids, fudging on the income tax, bitterness, anger, gossip, etc., etc.—God is tenacious in his commitment to developing us into people of integrity who love him, reflect him to others, and delight in doing his will.

—MARILYN MEBERG

Isn't It Nice to Know He Has a Sense of Humor?

G od is about as outrageous as life gets. When I was a child and I got stung by a bee or a zit exploded on my face, I would mutter under my breath, indicting Eve for throwing open the door to every petty ill that clouded my small world. Now as I have eased into my forties, I'm convinced I would have fallen as fast and as hard as she did because I'm no different from her. Each one of us has the same bent toward rebellion. And yet knowing that, knowing all of that, God made us.

—SHEILA WALSH

A lot of things changed during the eleven years my son Larry was [estranged from me], and the biggest change occurred in me. God changed my heart of stone into a heart of flesh, and I realized that God still loved Larry, no matter what he'd done—just as he still loved me, no matter what sins I'd committed. Some people think it's outrageous, but the truth is, as someone said, God loves all the flowers, even the wild ones that grow on the side of the road.

—BARBARA JOHNSON

God Made Us Just the Way We Are...

Everything comes from you, LORD, and we have given
you only what comes from your hand.

1 CHRONICLES 29:14

God chose to give us birth through the
word of truth, that we might be a kind
of firstfruits of all he created.

JAMES 1:18

Lord, you know all things; you
know that I love you.

JOHN 21:17

Isn't It Nice to Know He Has a Sense of Humor?

Everybody experiences difficult situations in life. Everybody. Things that make us want to scream out or give up. Deprivations. Sacrifices. Losses. Misunderstandings. But isn't there some way for the Christian to respond without getting mad at God? Otherwise, what's the good of our faith? There has to be some key to being joyful in the midst of discouraging circumstances and crabby people. What is it?

It's taking God at his Word. It's believing he will do what he says, no matter how things look or how we feel. Trusting God with everything we have, everything we are, every problem that is ours, every loss we endure, every battle we face, every person who disappoints us—with thanksgiving—gives us the grace to come through it with flying colors.

—Luci Swindoll

I feel best about myself, not when I read a flattering review of one of my books or when I am wearing a new outfit, but when I have selflessly reached out to someone in need and given without thought of reward—or of self. It is only when my self is submerged that God's image begins to shine forth. Then I have a healthy self-image that truly reflects God's image.

—Ruth A. Tucker

God Made Us Just the Way We Are...

It's hard to believe the Lord has trusted me with his ministry. There's no doubt that Christ Jesus really did go out on a limb—I'm talkin' way out there on a limb—when he allowed me to write books and be a speaker.

Speaking is the scariest thing I've ever done. I almost always get sick beforehand. Each time, I swear I'll never do it again. Added to that, I can't stand the sound of my voice. It's crotchety, exactly like my great aunt Annie's—God rest her soul—and I've never doubted for a minute I'm getting what my mother called my "just desserts." I'm being paid back for making fun of Aunt Annie behind her back!

Then there's the fact that no matter how hard I try, something always goes wrong.

In Chattanooga I was nearly dressed, and it was time to leave my hotel room for my speaking engagement when I discovered I hadn't brought my skirt.

In Pennsylvania I had both top and bottom of my two-piece dress, but, at the very last minute, found the dry cleaners had removed the buttons when they cleaned it and hadn't sewed them back on.

Isn't It Nice to Know He Has a Sense of Humor?

Another time I had what I thought was a pair of black high-heeled pumps, but they weren't a match; one had velvet trim and the other didn't. Then there's the time my slip fell down around my ankles just as I walked in front of the speaker's table.

So talk about God going out on a limb! He shows me off! Wow! Pretty amazing under the circumstances!

—SUE BUCHANAN

The development of a laugh attitude begins internally. It begins with a foundation that is God-inspired and God-constructed. That foundation gives us security as we stand confidently on the strength of God's incomparable love for each of us. The knowledge of that foundation then leads to personal rest and divine security.

—MARILYN MEBERG

God Made Us Just the Way We Are...

As long as I have life within me,
*   the breath of God in my nostrils,*
my lips will not speak wickedness,
*   and my tongue will utter no deceit.*

JOB 27:3-4

The LORD is my strength and my song;
*   he has become my salvation.*
He is my God, and I will praise him
*   my father's God, and I will exalt him.*

EXODUS 15:2

Our mouths were filled with laughter,
*   our tongues with songs of joy.*
Then it was said among the nations,
*   "The LORD has done great things for them."*

PSALM 126:2

Isn't It Nice to Know He Has a Sense of Humor?

So much of life is going, going, going, and doing, doing, doing, but we don't have to do everything ourselves. We can ask for help . . . if we're willing to let go of our demand to be in control and our desire to impress others (even God?) with our superhuman efforts.

—Sheila Walsh

There's no escaping reality, but we all try in a million different ways. Some of us sublimate, others ignore, and many (like me) live in denial. I told Marilyn the other day, "Denial is my reality." She laughed, but there's truth in that and she knows it. There are numerous times when living in the present is way too difficult, even though I am completely committed to the concept and preach it every chance I get. Like almost everything, it's easier said than done.

—Luci Swindoll

Hope is acting on the conviction that despite what we see with the natural eye, God is working in the spiritual realm to accomplish his perfect will in our lives. His hope does not disappoint!

—Thelma Wells

God Made Us Just the Way We Are...

A s I feel myself struggling to cope with unexpected trials, I see my heart as having, as part of its standard equipment, a zipper down the middle. On the left side is all my humanness—my selfish thoughts and inclinations, my anger, my resentments, etc. On the other side of the zipper is my spiritual side. It is from that side I determine to behave in ways I know to be kind, unselfish, and gracious, as well as to reflect the fruit of the Spirit.

However, when the left side of my heart becomes noisy and belligerent, I have to sit down and talk to it out of the right side. Unfortunately, sometimes that seems an unending dialogue. But eventually resolution is reached ... until the next time. As long as I am human, I am going to have a yacky, complaining left-of-the-zipper side. But God takes that side as well as my more spiritually developed side and embraces me, encourages me, listens to me, and never ceases to love me. He is, after all, my Father, whichever side of my zippered heart has the upper hand at that moment. And that thought brings me great joy and a cheerful heart.

—MARILYN MEBERG

Isn't It Nice to Know He Has a Sense of Humor?

I have been crucified with Christ and I no
longer live, but Christ lives in me. The life I live in
the body, I live by faith in the Son of God, who
loved me and gave himself for me.

GALATIANS 2:20

I am the LORD,
who has made all things,
who alone stretched out the heavens,
who spread out the earth by myself.

ISAIAH 44:24

My soul finds rest in God alone;
*   my salvation comes from him.*

PSALM 62:1

God Made Us Just the Way We Are...

Trust the heavenly Father of goodness. Giggle at his artistic genius in the world. Always remember you're created unique—just like everyone else!

—BARBARA JOHNSON

When we share the Bible with others, we are giving them life . . . wonderful words of life! We're not just making suggestions for living; we're offering individuals a new way to think, act, feel, and live. It's not here a verse, there a verse. In context, it's a new way to understand life. God's way.

—LUCI SWINDOLL

As you look back over the circumstances of your life, can you discern the carefully planned patterns that at first looked like coincidences? Situations don't always follow our plans, but God orchestrates our lives nonetheless—sometimes to a tune we hear only faintly.

—THELMA WELLS

Isn't It Nice to Know He Has a Sense of Humor?

S omeone once wrote me, "Sometimes I'm up; sometimes I'm down. I wish I could bottle feeling good and take a dose when I'm down." Not a single one of us has the luxury of giving up! With God, you reenter the arena of your fear, your failing, or your fatigue. No matter how you feel, dig your toes deep right now into the truth of Psalm 37:4. God will give you your heart's desire. He said it; it's true.

—BARBARA JOHNSON

Y ou can treat your enemies with love and respect even as they mistreat you. You can love your neighbors as you love yourself, even if they throw trash in your yard and yell at your children. You can forgive the ugly things people have done and said to you, and pardon them as God has pardoned you. No, it's not easy. But the practice of perfect makes perfect. Start practicing today by asking God to remove all the blocks that have kept you from forgiving and loving people.

—THELMA WELLS

God Made Us Just the Way We Are...

Teach me your way, O LORD,
and I will walk in your truth;
give me an undivided heart,
that I may fear your name.

PSALM 86:11

This is what the LORD says—
"Fear not, for I have redeemed you;
I have summoned you by name; you are mine."

ISAIAH 43:1

I pray that out of God's glorious riches he may
strengthen you with power through his Spirit
in your inner being so that Christ may dwell
in your hearts through faith. And I pray that you,
being rooted and established in love, may have power,
together with all the saints, to grasp how wide and
long and high and deep is the love of Christ.

EPHESIANS 3:16-18

Isn't It Nice to Know He Has a Sense of Humor?

The last time I ordered new glasses I had no-glare coating put on the lenses. That way, when I'm on a platform speaking, I don't refract light like some kind of Star Wars invader every time I turn my head. That no-glare stuff really works great, but as in most enhancements, there is a side effect—my lenses smudge easily. In fact, I'm constantly viewing life through thumbprints, which eliminates a lot of life's little details like steps, curbs, and hedges.

There are some advantages in not seeing clearly, you know. I mean, even the little I can see clearly in the morning mirror hasn't been all that wonderful. To see clearly could be more of a reality check than I'm ready for. If my house truly came into focus, I might have to do something radical—like vacuum. Not to mention the obligation I'd feel to weed the garden, wash the windows, and polish the silver. Nah, on second thought, who needs new glasses?

—Patsy Clairmont

God Made Us Just the Way We Are...

One day my phone rang, and the woman on the line identified herself as one who had heard a tape of mine on authenticity. She decided we might enjoy each other so she gave me a call. I discovered she was a speaker and writer herself and that her husband pastored a church in Newport Beach, California. I was flattered, as well as delighted, with the warmth and spontaneity of her overture. Within thirty minutes I was sure I had met one of those rare souls with whom I could be real. Within a few weeks I tested her by saying something I felt was true, but was nevertheless outrageous. There was a slight pause in the conversations, and I was afraid I had offended her when seconds later she said, "Marilyn—I can't believe you said that, but I couldn't agree more. I just wish I could quote you!" I am greatly enriched as this relationship grows and self-disclosure becomes increasingly effortless.

One of the serious consequences of perpetually masking and being phony is that it affects how we relate to God. How many times have we approached the Lord in prayer, careful to put our best spiritual foot forward? It's as if God didn't know that in reality we didn't feel like praying—we'd

Isn't It Nice to Know He Has a Sense of Humor?

rather be reading a book, playing tennis, drinking tea, chatting with a friend, or staring at a blank wall. Psalm 51:6 says, "Surely you desire truth in the inner parts; you teach me wisdom in the inmost place." God is asking me to approach him as I am—truthfully, honestly, without a pious mask.

—MARILYN MEBERG

The more a person has experienced the liberating love and acceptance of Christ, the more freedom she can welcome in others.

—PATSY CLAIRMONT

God Made Us Just the Way We Are...

Rich and poor have this in common:
The LORD is the Maker of them all.

PROVERBS 22:2

The God who made the world and everything
in it is the Lord of heaven and earth and does not live
in temples built by hands. And he is not served
by human hands, as if he needed anything, because he
himself gives all men life and breath and everything
else. God did this so that men would seek him
and perhaps reach out for him and find him,
though he is not far from each one of us. "For in
him we live and move and have our being."

ACTS 17:24-25, 27-28

The earth is the LORD's, and everything in it,
the world, and all who live in it.

PSALM 24:1

Isn't It Nice to Know He Has a Sense of Humor?

When we take refuge in God, he promises us peace beyond human comprehension. Every situation is included. So don't be afraid. There's no battle too fierce for God!

—THELMA WELLS

For years I've carried a little rock in my luggage everywhere I go. It's been my handy ammunition, a missile to throw at those who make mistakes. To be honest, I've considered throwing that old rock away; after all, it adds extra weight to my luggage. But I never know when I might need it.

I continue to carry that little rock with me everywhere I travel, but now it's not ammo; it's God's gracious reminder that I have a choice about how to respond to those who mistreat me. God has given me outrageous freedom; I'm free at any time to hurl stones of condemnation at the sinners around me . . . just as soon as I become sinless myself.

—BARBARA JOHNSON

The most profound truth in the universe is that God loves me; yet many miss that truth because of its simplicity.

—MARILYN MEBERG

God Made Us Just the Way We Are...

G race. It's a beautiful word, but I've struggled most of my life to wrap my heart around grace while trying to be perfect. Of course, perfection isn't the path to grace at all. Instead, attempted perfection (the only kind we can achieve) moves us further away from grace rather than toward it.

—SHEILA WALSH

W hat greater testimony can we give an unbelieving world than a cheerful, joyful demeanor that bespeaks an unshakable faith in the provision of an almighty God? That attitude says far more to others than any number of words and phrases we might offer in the vain hope that we are being a positive witness.

—MARILYN MEBERG

B eing a clownlike gal with my impish ways, I could be a little partial, but I think it's more than clowns' comical attire, their water-filled flowers, or their bulbous horns (honk!) that endear them to the world. I think the big appeal is their outrageous freedom to play the fool, the mime, the juggler, the victim, the hero, the Keystone cop, or the lost waif. Yes, a clown can be whomever she chooses, not only without opposition but also to rousing applause.

—PATSY CLAIRMONT

Isn't It Nice to Know He Has a Sense of Humor?

Since we live by the Spirit,
let us keep in step with the Spirit.

GALATIANS 5:25

Shout for joy, O heavens;
rejoice, O earth;
burst into song, O mountains!
For the LORD comforts his people
and will have compassion on his afflicted ones.

ISAIAH 49:13

I have hidden your word in my heart, O LORD,
that I might not sin against you.

PSALM 119:11

God Made Us Just the Way We Are...

We, as believers, know Jesus is no pit bull. He is, however, vigilant and never takes his eyes off us, not because he wants to catch us at something, but because his love for us causes him to watch out for the well-being of his children. One of the ways he has provided for our well-being is by giving us the capacity to be of good cheer. He has created within each of us a facility, even a giftedness, for being cheerful.

We are not talking about an ability to create humor. Not all people can do that. But all people can develop a cheerful interior. It's an attitude, a way of seeing life, that we can train ourselves to have. For life doesn't always give us a long list of reasons to be cheerful.

—MARILYN MEBERG

God never tells us to do anything that is impossible to do. What he says may not make complete sense to us, but it is good sense to do it anyway.

—THELMA WELLS

Isn't It Nice to Know He Has a Sense of Humor?

In my view, our worst enemy today is not unbelief, but legalism. It is that thing in us that wants to tell everybody else what to do, how to live, when to respond, and where to enlist. That is not our right. Instead, we have the responsibility to extend the grace and love of Christ to others so they don't stay tangled up in the ropes of slavery.

—LUCI SWINDOLL

I've discovered that when I finally throw myself out there in total abandonment to God, I'm never the same again. For me, learning to trust myself totally into the hands of God has helped me to trust others also.

Think of your own life. Stop for a moment and reflect on any situation where it seemed as if you were on your own, that it was hopeless, that you were forgotten. Remember how you could never have anticipated God showing up, but he did, with flying colors—even if it seemed like he left you dangling just a little too long for comfort!

—SHEILA WALSH

God Made Us Just the Way We Are...

The amazing thing about God's love is that he can be boilin' mad without losing his love for us even when "mostly we don't want to" do the right thing. He doesn't stop loving us even when we actually do the wrong thing. But God's love is not like cotton candy—sweet, cheap, and easy to digest. It cost him everything, and its demands on us can be hard to swallow. In response to his love, we are called to love as well: love him, love our neighbors, love our enemies—outrageously.

—MARILYN MEBERG

When we open God's Word, we hear Yahweh speak—the personal God of the Hebrew people who declared his existence to them so many centuries ago.

Take a few minutes today to spend with Yahweh. Find the comfort and guidance you need from God's words of direction for that disturbing circumstance in your life. His words are there, and they're written just for you.

—LUCI SWINDOLL

Isn't It Nice to Know He Has a Sense of Humor?

We can't change these seven realities:

Things are always changing. It rains on the just and the unjust. We are aging by the minute. The rules aren't fair. You can't please all people all the time. You can't heal another person's wounds. God is good anyway.

How often we need to be reminded that, regardless of our circumstances, God is constantly being good.

—BARBARA JOHNSON

How often do we ignore God's rules for our lives because we're too busy, too involved in our own thing, don't believe, make up your own rules, or choose to be downright rebellious? I can imagine God looking at us and saying, "My child, how many times does it take to convince you that my way is the right way? My timing is the perfect timing? My authority is the ultimate authority? My instructions will lead you to a way that has been designed for your good. Why don't you obey me?"

As he questions us, if we're sensitive to listen to his admonishment, we're quick to say, "Father, I'm sorry!" Before the twinkling of an eye, he says, "Forgiven!"

—THELMA WELLS

God Made Us Just the Way We Are...

He brought me out into a spacious place;
he rescued me because he delighted in me.

PSALM 18:19

It's mind-boggling to most of us that the God of the universe actually delights in us, but Scripture says he does. We first have to underscore the tremendous love and delight God feels for us before we even begin to grasp the magnitude of what he overcame on the cross. His love sent Jesus to the cross; knowing he delights in us allows us to feel secure about who we are and whose we are. I'll have to say in all candor, I struggle daily with my inability to comprehend God's boundless, unconditional, and even relentless love for me.

—MARILYN MEBERG

I am no Pollyanna. I don't believe in burying my head in the sand. I like to face life head-on and deal with it. Having said that, I refuse to get caught up in the spirit of despair that is seeping through the world and creeping into the church. We look at world events, the economy, the chaos, and we become filled with fear of the days that lie ahead, as if God hadn't read the latest edition of "Time" magazine before he gave us his Word. It's just that from this side of the cloth, we can't see the whole picture.

—SHEILA WALSH

Isn't It Nice to Know He Has a Sense of Humor?

Be joyful always; pray continually.

1 Thessalonians 5:16–17

The Lord must have had busy women in mind when he said to pray continually. We have to pray continually just to get through the day! It's a good thing God didn't say we had to stop five times (or seven, or even once), run to the bedroom, and get down on our knees by the bed, or our prayers wouldn't count. If he had, most of us wouldn't do it. Another thing—he must have taken into consideration the fact that while we were off praying our kids would be off killing each other!

Unless I'm misinterpreting the verse, I think it's implying that praying continually will make us joyful. It occurs to me that if I'm really praying continually, then maybe this attitude of joy will spill over into my activities and behaviors, and maybe even back into my prayers!

—Sue Buchanan

God Made Us Just the Way We Are...

He is the image of the invisible God, the firstborn
over all creation. For by him all things were created:
things in heaven and on earth, visible and invisible,
whether thrones or powers or rulers or authorities;
all things were created by him and for him.

Colossians 1:15-16

You are worthy, our Lord and God,
  to receive glory and honor and power,
for you created all things,
  and by your will they were created
  and have their being.

Revelation 4:11

Isn't It Nice to Know He Has a Sense of Humor?

I have an appreciation for the imperative of coming to God with an honest heart rather than a mask. God doesn't minister to the phony front. He sees behind our masks, and he longs to love, comfort, and sustain us. We need to be real with him.

—MARILYN MEBERG

God used common folks for the most sacred, esteemed assignment in human history: the birth of his only begotten Son. Jesus' birth was a consummate example of the extraordinary swaddled in the ordinary. And God, in his outrageous love, continues to use ordinary people—you and me—to ring in his kingdom today.

—THELMA WELLS

I don't think it's possible to be a cheerful overcomer without the sure foundation of knowing God loves me exactly as I am once I have received forgiveness for sin. I can't do anything to win him, impress him, or further convince him I am worthy of his love and delight.

—MARILYN MEBERG

Sources

Sue Buchanan, *Duh-votions: Words of Wisdom for the Spiritually Challenged* (Grand Rapids, MI: Zondervan Publishing House, 1999).

Marilyn Meberg, *Choosing the Amusing* (Nashville, TN: Word Publishing, 1999). *I'd Rather Be Laughing* (Nashville, TN: Word Publishing, 1998).

Thelma Wells, Sheila Walsh, et al, *Outrageous Joy: the Life-Changing, Soul-Shaking Truth About God* (Grand Rapids, MI: Zondervan Publishing House, 1999). *Overjoyed! Devotions to Tickle Your Fancy and Strengthen Your Faith* (Grand Rapids, MI: Zondervan Publishing House, 1999).